HOW CAN I HELP DURING COVID-19?

Bookmobile
Fountaindale Public Library
Bolingbrook, IL
(630) 759-2102

By Emily Dolbear

The Child's World®

childsworld.com

Published by The Child's World®
1980 Lookout Drive
Mankato, MN 56003-1705
800-599-READ
www.childsworld.com

Photos ©: BlurryMe/Shutterstock.
com: 16; Chernyshkova
Natalia/Shutterstock.com: 19;
DeeMPhotography/Shutterstock.
com: 10; GrandeDuc/Shutterstock.
com: 5; Kues/Shutterstock.com: 9;
Kzenon/Shutterstock.com: Laboo
Studio/Shutterstock.com: 15;
Ralf Geithe/Shutterstock.com: 6;
VCoscaron/Shutterstock.com: 13;
Volurol/Shutterstock.com: cover, 2

ISBN 9781503852778
(Reinforced Library Binding)

ISBN 9781503853195
(Portable Document Format)

ISBN 9781503853256
(Online Multi-user eBook)

LCCN: 2020939107

Printed in the United
States of America

About the Author

Emily J. Dolbear writes
and edits books from
her home in Brookline,
Massachusetts. She
lives with her family
and their dog, who has
provided much comfort
during COVID-19.

CONTENTS

CHAPTER ONE
A New Virus   4

CHAPTER TWO
Doing Your Part   11

CHAPTER THREE
What Else Can I Do?   18

Think about It   21
Good News!   22
Glossary   23
To Learn More   24
Index   24

A New Virus

Germs are tiny living things all around us. You need a special microscope to see them. One type of germ is a **virus**. Like many germs, a virus inside your body can make you sick. Viruses cause colds, the flu, and measles.

In 2019, a new virus appeared in central China. It made many people sick with a disease called COVID-19. That's short for "**CO**rona **VI**rus **D**isease 20**19**." **Coronaviruses** are a group of viruses that can **infect** animals and humans. Scientists do not know the exact source of this new coronavirus.

Coronavirus cells are shaped like spiky balls. The spikes break into healthy cells in the body.

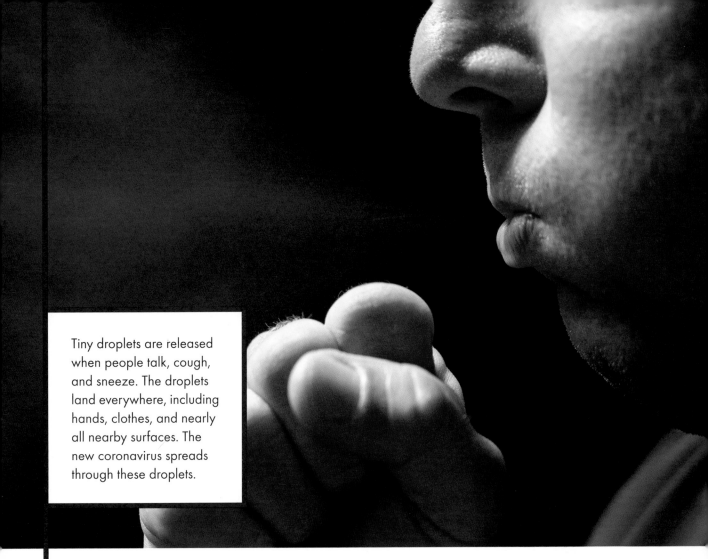

Tiny droplets are released when people talk, cough, and sneeze. The droplets land everywhere, including hands, clothes, and nearly all nearby surfaces. The new coronavirus spreads through these droplets.

There is still much to learn about COVID-19. One thing scientists know for sure is that the virus is very **contagious**. That means it spreads easily between people. COVID-19 spread quickly in the first half of 2020. Millions of people around the world became ill.

Vaccines can prevent the spread of deadly diseases. A vaccine has small amounts of weak or dead germs. Getting a vaccine helps protect you from certain diseases. Work on a COVID-19 vaccine has already started.

This virus has changed our daily lives in many ways. You may feel anxious. You may wonder how you can help during COVID-19.

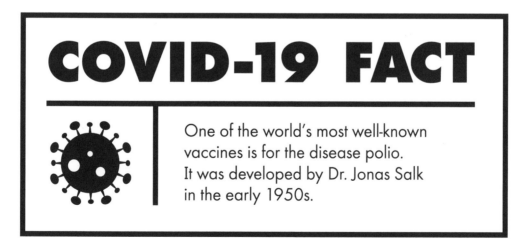

COVID-19 FACT

One of the world's most well-known vaccines is for the disease polio. It was developed by Dr. Jonas Salk in the early 1950s.

The first step is to understand how the virus spreads. Most of the time, one person passes it to another. A cough or sneeze sprays tiny drops. Those drops can land in other people's mouths, noses, or eyes. That's how germs enter the body. And that is how the virus spreads.

Those with COVID-19 may have a cough. It might be hard for them to breathe. They may also have a fever or a sore throat. It is possible for an infected person who feels okay or just a little sick to spread the virus.

Some people say their COVID-19 symptoms felt like a common cold at first.

Any type of soap will kill the coronavirus germs. So choose your favorite!

CHAPTER TWO

Doing Your Part

Kids can do their part to stop the spread of the virus. The best way to stay healthy is washing your hands. That prevents the passing of germs to other people. Make it a habit after using the bathroom and before you eat.

Handwashing may seem easy. But there are some helpful rules. You must wet your hands, use soap, and lather. Remember to wash between your fingers. The backs of your hands need cleaning too. It should take about 20 seconds. That's as long as it takes to hum the "Happy Birthday" song twice. Then rinse and dry your hands.

COVID-19 FACT

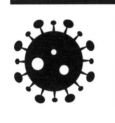

Did you know there's a day to celebrate the importance of clean hands in the prevention of diseases? October 15 has been Global Handwashing Day since 2008.

Another way to stop a virus from spreading is to stay away from sick people. But it isn't always easy to know who is infected with COVID-19. That is why physical distancing helps.

Physical distancing is keeping space between you and others outside your home. That means staying away from large groups and crowded places. This may mean not being with friends or neighbors.

Visiting with friends and family over a computer, smartphone, or tablet is a great way to stay connected.

You may miss seeing some family members in person. While this is hard, it's not forever. It's how you can help during the time of COVID-19.

You can do your part in other ways. Wearing a face mask prevents the spread of the virus. Put on a cloth face cover when you have to go out. Stay at least 6 feet (2 meters) away from people in public places. This helps prevent the passing on of any germs.

It's best to wear the mask snugly. It should go over your nose and under your chin. You can remove the mask when you are back home again.

COVID-19 FACT

Masks mostly help to keep the wearer's germs from spreading to others. They only help a little to keep the wearer safe from germs that are already in the air.

Masks can be paper or cloth. They can be purchased from a store or even homemade.

Coughing or sneezing into your elbow stops many of the droplets that might otherwise end up in the air.

Covering your mouth and nose during a cough or sneeze is always a good idea. You can use a tissue. Be sure to throw the used tissue away. Then wash your hands. If necessary, sneeze in the inside of your elbow.

If you don't have soap and water, you can use hand sanitizer. Rub it all over your hands. Let them air dry. Do your part to clean germs from the surfaces around you. Use soap and water.

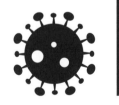

Americans first used disposable tissues in 1924. They used tissues to remove facial cream. Now everyone uses tissues when they sneeze.

CHAPTER THREE

What Else Can I Do?

During the time of COVID-19, school districts sent students home. Public buildings of all kinds closed. Special events like birthday parties and concerts were canceled. Many adults began working from home. People stopped going to the movies. They weren't able to eat any meals in restaurants.

Helping others can make us feel better during difficult times. How can you help out at home? You could offer to set the table. Or make your bed. Or ask someone in your family to go for a walk. You could take care of any pets in your home.

Making masks to give away to others is a great way to help during COVID-19.

You can help people outside your home too. Even though you may not be able to visit in person, you can still connect. Make a video call to friends who you miss. Send a note in the mail. Older and younger family members will appreciate hearing from you. Your classmates will be happy you thought of them.

The world around us changed quickly during this time. Your family is there to support you. Get the latest information from your local authorities. Learn more about staying healthy and doing your part. Remember to do fun things with your family too. There is much you can do to help during COVID-19.

THINK ABOUT IT

There are lots of things you can do at home while keeping yourself and others safe.

1. Do you know anyone with a birthday soon? Think of a way to celebrate that person from a distance.

2. Find out about homemade face masks. Perhaps you could use things around your home. Ask for help to make one for a neighbor.

3. Create a small poster with handwashing tips. Post it near the bathroom sink. It will remind your family members of the importance of clean hands.

GOOD NEWS!

There has been some good news during COVID-19. Some animal-loving families have helped others and themselves. They have taken in stray animals. This extra time at home is perfect for bonding with a new cat or dog.

An animal rescue group in New York City reported its most pet adoptions in a month. A shelter in Palm Beach County, Florida, found homes for dozens of dogs. April 2020 was the first time the animal shelter had completely emptied a kennel.

But the need for animal shelters is not over. There will always be animals in need of a caring home.

GLOSSARY

contagious (kun-TAY-juss) If something is contagious, it spreads easily between people.

coronaviruses (kah-ROHN-uh-VY-ruh-sez) A coronavirus can infect animals and humans. COVID-19 is caused by a coronavirus.

infect (in-FEKT) To infect is to cause disease by introducing a virus.

vaccines (vak-SEENZ) A vaccine is a weakened or dead form of a disease that is swallowed or injected into a person. This causes their body to fight the germs, and gives them the ability to fight that disease's germs if the body comes in contact with them again.

virus (VY-russ) A virus is a very tiny germ that causes diseases. A virus can only be seen with a special kind of microscope.

TO LEARN MORE

IN THE LIBRARY

Alber, Diane. *A Little SPOT Stays Home: A Story About Viruses And Safe Distancing.* Diane Alber Art, LLC, 2020.

Squire, Ann O. *Flu.* New York, NY: Scholastic, 2016.

Wallace, Adam M. *The Day My Kids Stayed Home: Explaining COVID-19 and the Corona Virus to Your Kids.* Adam M. Wallace, 2020.

ON THE WEB

Visit our website for links about COVID-19:

childsworld.com/links

Note to Parents, Teachers, and Librarians: We routinely verify our Web links to make sure they are safe and active sites. So encourage your readers to check them out!

INDEX

coronaviruses, 4, 5, 6, 10
coughing, 6, 8, 16. 17
COVID-19 name, 4
hand washing, 11, 12, 17, 21

helping out, 18, 19, 20, 21
masks, 14, 15, 19, 21
physical distancing, 12, 13, 14

sanitizer, 17
spreading, 6, 7, 8, 11, 12, 14
vaccines, 7